Shapes & Patterns
IN NATURE

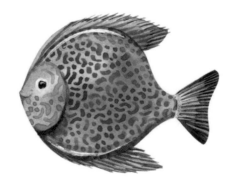

Albatros

Contents

Prelude

In autumn, the ground is covered in leaves of all shapes and sizes. Some are round like a palm, others resemble a heart, and yet others are adorned with waves or prickly serrations. In the middle of each leaf, nature has fixed a pattern of tiny veins that is unique to that particular leaf, just like our fingerprints are unique to us. There is a reason plants, animals, and minerals have diverse shapes and colorful patterns—it's all very important.

Play of shapes

Leaves of sunflowers, as large as tiny sails, catch more light from the sun, and the narrow leaves of conifers, called nettles, are better for handling the wind when there's a savage storm.

Hide-and-seek

Plants and animals use their motley range of shapes and patterns to communicate. Whenever anyone needs a good spooking, dangerous-looking black-and-yellow stripes will definitely work. In winter, the careful brown stoat does wonders with its snow-white camouflage, which allows it to frolic in the snow without a care in the world. And what does the stick insect above mask itself as?

Chameleon, master of disguise

Some animals can change their patterns just like that, depending on their mood. A chameleon, for example, has three layers of miniature skin cells with a colorful pigment. When these cells mix, the little monkey brightens up in surprise, contentment, or annoyance. When tired, it turns pale green. And when in love, its body lights up with the most beautiful colors.

Repetition in nature

Have you noticed that some shapes and patterns occur again and again in nature? Long ago, people relied on them to try and understand the invisible order of the wilderness. And today, mathematicians can accurately express some of these mysterious patterns in mathematical equations.

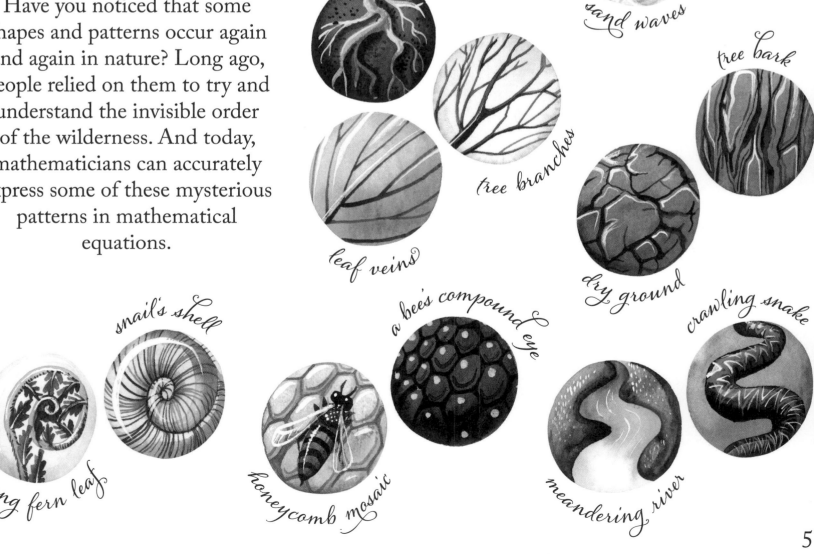

ocean waves

sand waves

tree roots

tree branches

tree bark

leaf veins

dry ground

crawling snake

snail's shell

a bee's compound eye

young fern leaf

honeycomb mosaic

meandering river

carrot

garden rocket

sunflower

true lavender

string-of-pearls

lettuce

Savoy cabbage

field salad

peppermint

yarrow

hosta

red currant

red clover

wild strawberry

spiny leaf insect

common nettle

ribwort plantain

wood sorrel

plumeless thistle

lady's mantle

male fern

lance-shaped

ovale

cordate

spathulate

pinnatisect

pinnate

6

Leaves

Leaves catch rays of sunshine in their green palms so that they can grow and live happily. Whether they're broad, narrow, pointed, or heart-shaped, all fulfill their purpose. When the dry season comes they would rather fall than see their beloved plant go thirsty.

common ivy

bamboo

coconut tree

agave

Monstera deliciosa

common grape vine

common houseleek

hedge bedstraw

peacock plant

heather

birch

linden

larch needles

wood violet

dandelion

horse-chestnut

beech

black locust

oak

ginkgo

maple

trifoliate

whorled

rosette

alternate

palmate

bipinnate

7

beech

oak

juniper

black poplar

Manchurian striped maple

wild cherry

quaking aspen

Scots pine

apple tree

eucalyptus

Norway spruce

littleleaf linden

American sycamore

flowering dogwood

silk floss tree

sycamore maple

silver birch

Scots pine

oak

Norway spruce

white willow

rainbow eucalyptus

hornbeam

8

Tree bark

Rough bark is to a tree what skin is to a human. It protects a tree's sap-filled vessels from the burning sun, the lashing rain and the frost of winter. As years pass, wrinkles and cracks pile on, peeling to reveal young bark quietly awaiting its turn. It is ready to age and take care of its tree.

oil palm

banana plant

coral bark maple

baobab

cork oak

birch bark cherry

banyan fig

rainbow eukalyptus

teak

Natchez crape myrtle

silver birch

white willow

tea tree

oil palm

banyan fig

juniper

wild cherry

cork oak

banana plant

9

lantana

ranunculus

autumn crocus

daisy

purple dragon

honeysuckle

fuchsia

fox geranium

wood forget-me-not

camellia

edelweiss

blanket flower

goldenrod

Miss Willmott's ghost

bladder campion

ice plant

gerbera

red poppy

yellow toadflax

great masterwort

passion flower

butterbur

wild carrot

lesser periwinkle

snake's head fritillary

hellebore

giant onion

snowdrop

Solomon's seal

marsh spurge

Knautia macedonica

garden cosmos

wild pansy

cornflower

harebell

stellate

galeate

disc flowers (in the middle)

funnelform

campanulate

ray flowers

Flowers

Round, fluffy, or ruffled, striking or subdued—colorful blossoms lure insect suitors with their beauty. They shake their heads and butterflies go wild, digging their noses into fragrant cups, before taking off to spread pollen seeds throughout the land. Next year, as every year, there'll be a few more flowers.

flame lily

pitcher plant

elephant apple

spring starflower

flowering quince

Chinese hibiscus

moth orchid

jade vine

petunia

pink silk tree

bleeding heart

voodoo lily

cross-leaved heath

water lily

bird of paradise

monkey orchid

trumpet gentian

coltsfoot

tulip

dandelion

torch ginger

royal lily

silver vase plant

common sugarbrush

corpse lily

celosia

hyacinth

capitulum

cyme

head

spadix

compound umbel

panicle

11

watermelon

strawberry

pumpkin

papaya

radish

pomegranate

raspberry

lychee

rambutan

prickly pear

red currant

cantaloupe

lemon

beetroot

dragon fruit

mangosteen

apricot

fig

onion

tomato

carrot

chilli pepper

passion fruit

gooseberry

grapefruit

rhubarb

eggplant

garlic

cucumber

olives

berries

drupes

pomes

citruses

melons

tropical fruits

12

star fruit

pomelo

banana

lime

blueberries

avocado

apple

durian

asparagus

kiwi

Fruits & vegetables

Round, pointed, egg-shaped, or star-shaped.
Nature has gifted us all kinds of goodies with all kinds
of tastes. Care for a sweet apple, a sour kiwi, a hot
pepper with garlic, or a bitter asparagus? How about
a head of artichoke or a piece of scaly dragon fruit?
There's something for all taste buds!

guava

Brussels sprout

spinach

peas

grapes

artichoke

pepper

zucchini

romanesco broccoli

root vegetables

fruit vegetables

leafy green vegetables

allium vegetables

cruciferous vegetables

pod vegetables

cashews

walnuts

sunflower seeds

acorn

old man's beard seeds

linden seeds

almonds

hazelnut

sycamore seeds

chestnut

juniper cones

star anise seeds

vanilla pod

beech nuts

ash samaras

hop seed cones

beans

dill seeds

spruce cone

bald cypress cone

poppy capsule

elephant-ear tree seedpod

black alder cones

elm samaras

cotton boll

dandelion achenes

acorn

pod

cone

single samaras

double samara

achenes

14

Nuts & seeds

Seeds aren't much to look at. Some fly through the air on a downy parachute, others fall straight to the fluffy ground—boom! All have one thing in common—their tiny bodies carry the germ of a new life and bravely spread it far and wide. Nuts and seeds, small and smaller still.

banksia seedpod

raffia nuts

Chinese lantern seedpods

annual honesty silicules

Cerbera odollam seed

nutmeg

quinoa grains

rice grains

coriander seeds

buckwheat grains

cocoa beans

macadamia nuts

tea mangrove seeds

catalpa bean pods

tea tree seedpods

maple samaras

red sandalwood pod

hornbeam samaras

willow tree seeds

wheat grains

lotus seed capsule

pine nuts

nut-like drupe

nuts in spiny bur

grains

nut

capsule

silicule

true tulip

pink conch

lettered olive

bubble shell

Tampa bay top snail

tiger cowrie

worm shell

Atlantic sundial

sunray venus clam

japanese volute

banded tulip

knobbed whelk

alphabet cone

American auger

junonia

fighting conch

lightning whelk

horse conch

Scotch bonnet

arrow dwarf triton

bay scallop

wentletrap

prickly cockle

lace murex

long spined star

dosinia

queen helmet

Cabrit's murex

yellow cockle

lion's paw scallop

oyster

sunray venus

Scotch bonnet

razor clam

cockle

shark eye

16

Shells

Home to soft mollusk bodies, they dazzle the world with their uncommon beauty. Chalky shells that look like two conjoined bowls are created by smaller mollusks, like oysters, clams, and mussels. Larger but no less fragile mollusks, such as snails and slugs, protect themselves in shells shaped like spirals.

Roman snail

grove snail

common nutmeg shell

giant African snail

angel wing

coquina clams

shark eye shell

keyhole sand dollar

baby's ear shell

turkey wing

razor clam

sea snail

nautilus shell

giant clam

pen shell

blue mussel

hermit crab

chiton

thorny oyster

moon shell

oyster

common limpet

lightning whelk

coquina clam

scallop

American auger

dosinia

tulip shell

small green awlet

yellow swallowtail

speckled wood

four-spotted chaser

marbled white

claudina butterfly

Spanish apple moth

spotted lanternfly

Spanish moon moth

luna moth

Picasso moth

sunset moth from Madagascar

regal moth

orange tip

emerald swallowtail

peacock butterfly

Madagascar moon moth

Rajah Brooke's birdwing

crimson rose butterfly

thorn bug

pink katydid

lace bug

owl moth

atlas moth

green tiger beetle

cockroaches

bees and wasps

dragonflies

walking sticks

cicadas

beetles

18

Insect wings & shards

In the dim and distant past, a piece of skin shot out of a butterfly's chest and turned into beautiful wings—colorful, showy, and striped, and covered with tiny scales stacked like roof tiles. But bugs hide their see-through wings beneath firm shards, so that they don't break.

beautiful demoiselle

Halloween pennant

plume moth

banded darter

poplar hawk-moth

white lined moth

banded demoiselle

tree wasp

orchid bee

marmalade hoverfly

glasswinged butterfly

spiny flower mantis

monarch butterfly

Kentish glory

Carabus ground beetle

seven-spot ladybird

blue walking stick

Italian striped bug

Picasso bug

burying beetle

potato beetle

small emperor moth

vineyard cicada

desert locust

brush jewel beetle

Papuan green weevil

cockroach

Alpine longhorn beetle

green milkweed grasshopper

red spotted jewel beetle

transparent butterfly wings

scaly butterfly wings

swallowtail wings

moth wings

plume moth wing

beetle elytra

19

rainbow kribensis

sixline wrasse

Jack Dempsey

harlequin rasboras

clown loach

red-spotted blenny

neon tetras

clownfish

ram cichlid

freshwater angelfish

moorish idol

fire goby

discus fish

guppy fish

clown triggerfish

porcupinefish

pearl danio

bluefin notho

swordtail

Banggai cardinalfish

orange head eartheater

deep-sea angler

common fangtooth

golden sailfin molly

red-tailed black shark

cycloid scales

placoid scales

pelvic fin

ctenoid scales

ganoid scales

dorsal fin

20

Fins & scales

Scales are like a fish's tree rings. Read them and know the age of the fish and where it has swum. Is this scale new or a thousand years old? Who cares! A fish, with or without scales, flaps its fins and disappears to the safety of the deep, beyond the curious human gaze.

paradise fish

blue Jack Dempsey

royal gramma

Siamese fighting fish

lionfish

jewel cichlid

threadfin butterflyfish

queen angelfish

zebra danios

Halfmoon Siamese fighting fish

electric yellow lab

Lagoon triggerfish

clown killifish

juvenile emperor angelfish

Endlers livebearers

annularis angelfish

dwarf seahorse

psychedelic frogfish

yellow boxfish

gold nugget pleco

fire eel

rounded tail fin

forked tail fin

crescendic tail fin

pointed tail fin

truncate tail fin

emarginate tail fin

draco lizard

mimic poison frog

tiger-striped leaf frog

Parsons' chameleon

albino tangerine milk snake

Mexican alligator lizard

tokay gecko

collared lizard

Augrabies flat lizard

reticulated glass frog

green and black dart frog

African egg-eating snake

blue-tailed skink

green iguana

pangolin

spiny-tailed monitor

horned toad

rhinoceros iguana

painted reed frog

corn snake

leopard frog

armadillo girdled lizard

roly-poly

coral snake

irregular scales

regular scales

mucronate scales

rectangular scales

polygonal scales

rhomboid scales

22

armadillo

veiled chameleon

panther chameleon

green thornytail iguana

green basilisk

Skin & carapaces

Without their skin, amphibians and reptiles would be naked. Horny skin keeps them from drying out and makes them look scary. When the time comes, they replace their old skin with new, like how we change coats. Snakes shed skin whole, lizards and turtles peel it off slowly. Turtles are like knights—armored with a shell that evolved from their ribs.

common green forest lizard

rhinoceros viper

Madagascar leaf-nosed snake

serrated tortoise

red-eared slider

leopard tortoise

Chinese water dragon

gharial

green anole

thorny devil

frilled lizard

dwarf crocodile

cycloid scales

rough crocodile skin

smooth frog skin

spiny scales

spiral-shaped carapace

starry-shaped carapace

resplendent quetzal

green-tailed sunbird

turquoise-browed motmot

blue jay

Taiwan magpie

great horned owl

Himalayan vulture

greater bird of paradise

ostrich

cedar waxwing

white-spotted fantail

red-headed trogon

crimson sunbird

black-naped tern

lilac breasted roller

Indian peafowl

sparrowhawk

African crowned crane

downy woodpecker

greater painted-snipe

wood duck

common loon

sandgrouse

down feather

contour feather

hummingbird feathers

wing feather

tail feather

semiplume feather

24

Bird wings & feathers

Feathers, feathers everywhere! Downy and contoured, every bird's pride. A layer of feathers shields birds from bitter frosts. Last but not least, feathers give most birds the power of flight. The lucky fellows simply flap their wings and off they go . . . up toward the sun.

golden-breasted starling

Wilson's bird of paradise

river kingfisher

fiery-throated hummingbird

white-throated mountaingem

common starling

Cuban tody

marvelous spatuletail

scissor-tailed flycatcher

Victoria crowned pigeon

golden pheasant

palm cockatoo

Himalayan monal

blood pheasant

blue-and-yellow macaw

bee-eater

keel-billed toucan

guineafowl

Schalow's turaco

Eurasian hoopoe

gliding wing

rapid takeoff wing

hovering wing

golden pheasant feathers

soaring wing

high-speed wing

cheetah

leopard

wildcat

zebra

springbok

reticulated giraffe

Masai giraffe

okapi

chipmunk

Barbary mouse

golden hamster

striped skunk

American bison

numbat

speckled ground squirrel

marbled polecat

fallow deer

fox

Dalmatian

Iberian lynx

Bengal tiger

samoyed

Afghan hound

striped fur

reticulated fur

stains

spots

dots

tabby fur

stoat in summer fur

stoat in winter fur

giant panda

red panda

brown long-eared bat

common genet

pale tussock caterpillar

sycamore moth caterpillar

flannel moth

ermine moth

bumblebee

cow

Suffolk sheep

Hungarian Racka sheep

Fur & hair

Thanks to its striped fur, a tiger can hide in the tall grass of the savannah, unseen, except maybe by the long-necked giraffe, which is proud of its spots. These spots aren't just for show, they regulate heat. Hair and fur, long, short, straight, or curly—animals couldn't do without it. And did you know that a hedgehog's spine, too, is a hair?

ocelot

Indian porcupine

Highland cow

Yeti crab

sea otter

Goliath birdeater

hedgehog

Mary River turtle

ringed seal

curly fur

wavy fur

wet fur

prickly fur

straight silky fur

fine hairs

27

laminated sandstone

rutile

tiger's eye

vanadinite

wulfenite

aragonite

crocoite

lightning agate

amber

little garnets

pyrite

aragonite balls

golden topaz

mica

conglomerate

rhodochrosite

ferric quartz

hematite

magnesite

pumice

chiastolite

sagenite

quartz

tourmaline

wollastonite

chalcopyrite

desert rose

natrolite

halite

bayldonite

moldavite

opal

wavellite

bismuth

pyromorphite

silver

granular aggregate

lamellar aggregate

bladed aggregate

needlelike aggregate

radiating aggregate

dendritic aggregate

28

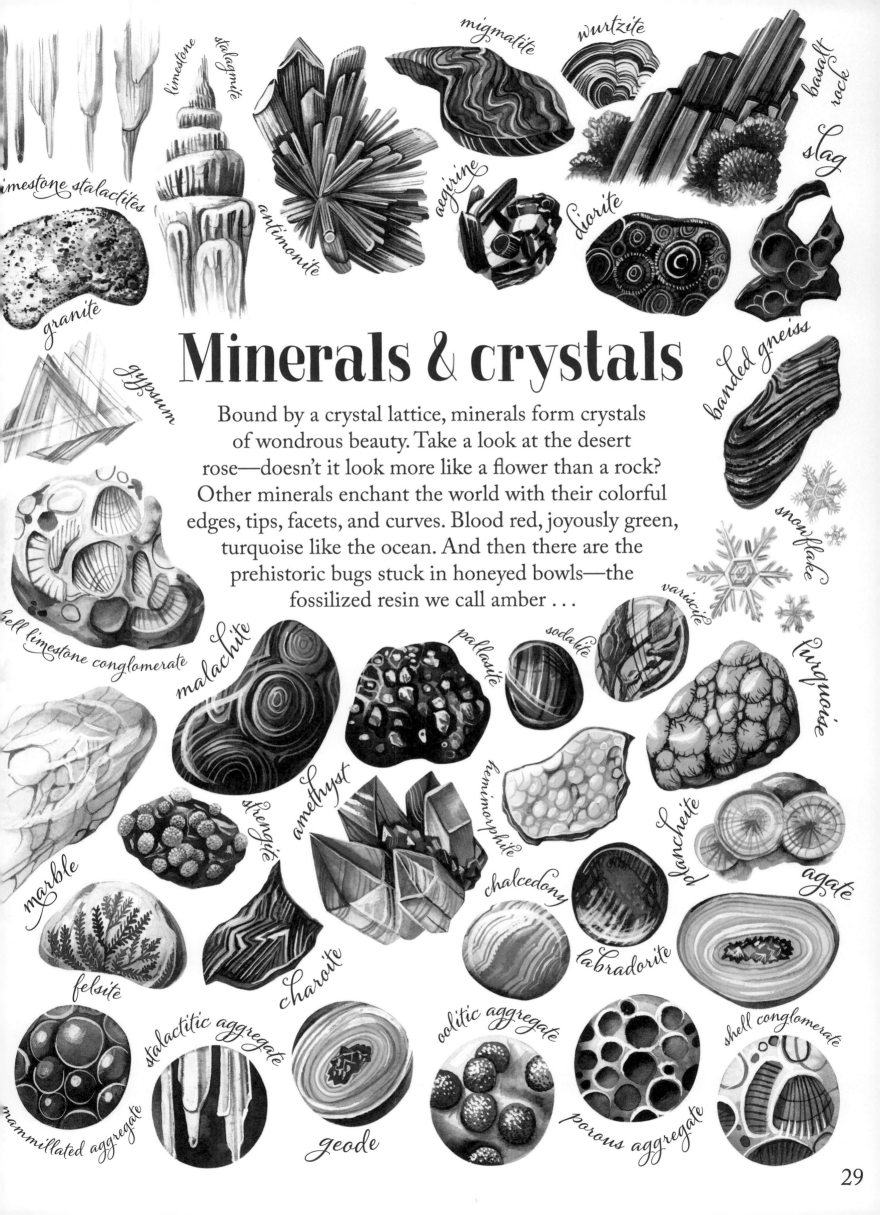

Minerals & crystals

Bound by a crystal lattice, minerals form crystals of wondrous beauty. Take a look at the desert rose—doesn't it look more like a flower than a rock? Other minerals enchant the world with their colorful edges, tips, facets, and curves. Blood red, joyously green, turquoise like the ocean. And then there are the prehistoric bugs stuck in honeyed bowls—the fossilized resin we call amber . . .

limestone stalactites

limestone stalagmite

antimonite

migmatite

wurtzite

geode or druse

aegirine

diorite

slag

granite

gypsum

banded gneiss

snowflake

variscite

shell limestone conglomerate

malachite

pallasite

sodalite

turquoise

marble

shengite

amethyst

hemimorphite

blancheite

agate

chalcedony

labradorite

felsite

charoite

mammillated aggregate

stalactitic aggregate

geode

oolitic aggregate

porous aggregate

shell conglomerate

29

A parade of patterns . . .

round

radish

raspberry

rutile

ringed seal

owl moth

wavy

giant clam

Kentish glory

rhinoceros viper

banyan fig

oak leaf

pointed

Indian porcupine

porcupinefish

pink conch

silver vase plant

thorny oyster

striped

nautilus shell

zebra

peacock plant

small green awlet

Italian striped bug

dotted and spotted

yellow boxfish

leopard

junonia

corpse lily

seven-spot ladybird

branched

lionfish

Cerbera odollam seed

spiny flower mantis

Chinese lantern seedpods

vineyard cicada

...and shapes

Can you find other plants, animals, and minerals with these shapes and patterns?

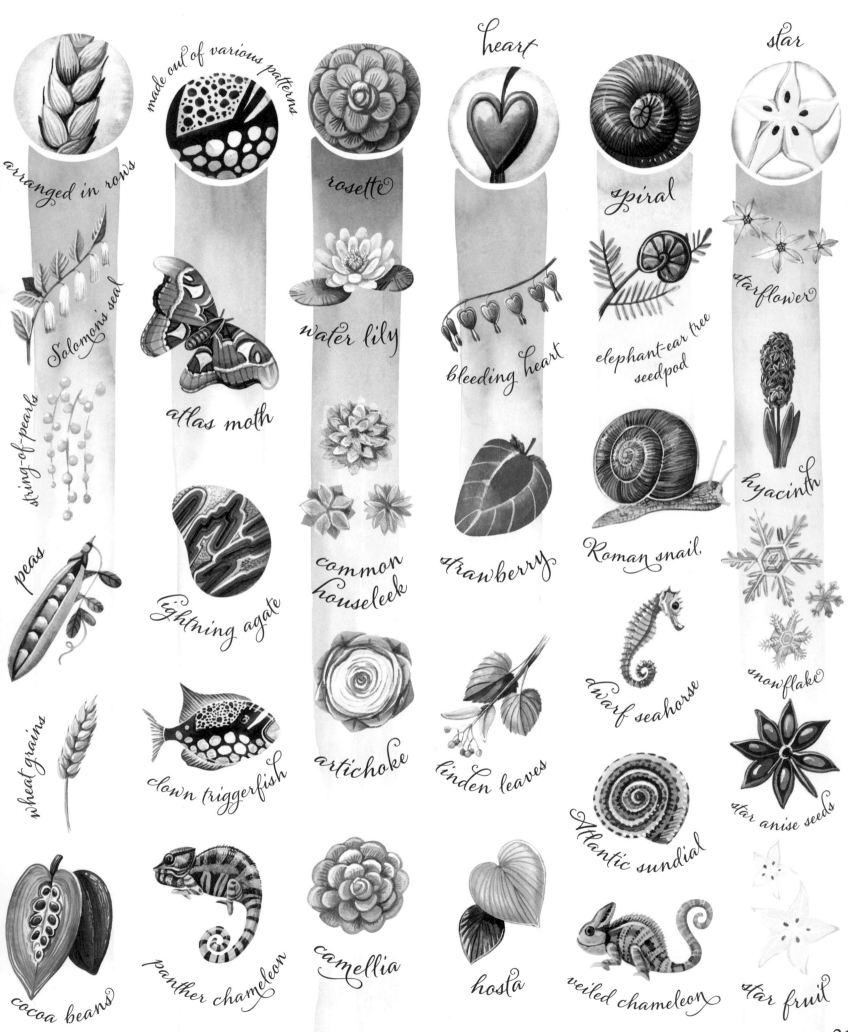

arranged in rows

Solomon's seal

string-of-pearls

peas

wheat grains

made out of various patterns

atlas moth

lightning agate

clown triggerfish

cocoa beans

panther chameleon

rosette

water lily

common houseleek

artichoke

camellia

heart

bleeding heart

strawberry

linden leaves

hosta

spiral

elephant-ear tree seedpod

Roman snail

dwarf seahorse

Atlantic sundial

veiled chameleon

star

starflower

hyacinth

snowflake

star anise seeds

star fruit

© B4U Publishing for Albatros,
an imprint of Albatros Media Group, 2021
5. května 1746/22, Prague 4, Czech Republic
Authors: Jana Sedláčková, Štěpánka Sekaninová
Illustrator: Magdalena Konečná
Printed in China by Leo Paper Group
ISBN: 978-80-00-06125-2